WELCOME

You are invited

to feel

your feelings

HERE...

Cover design, interior design and typesetting by Monica N. Ghali
Edited by Catherine Knepper

Author's Note

This publication is not intended as a substitute for the advice of
health care professionals.

THE GUEST HOUSE

This being human is a guest house.
Every morning a new arrival.

A joy, a depression, a meanness,
some momentary awareness comes
as an unexpected visitor.

Welcome and entertain them all!
Even if they're a crowd of sorrows,
who violently sweep your house
empty of its furniture,
still, treat each guest honorably.
He may be clearing you out
for some new delight.

The dark thought, the shame, the malice,
meet them at the door laughing, and invite them in.

Be grateful for whatever comes,
because each has been sent
as a guide from beyond.

Jelaluddin Rumi,
translation by Coleman Bark

PREFACE

You are invited to a feelings journal experience. The invitation is simply this—when you feel, *feel*.

How often are we inattentive to our feelings? How many times have we been afraid of the depth of our feelings? Are there moments when we push our feelings away? How frequently do we choose not to explore the meanings or messages of our feelings? How often are we afraid to actually *feel*—afraid that if we truly let the feelings flow we might not recover from the crying, from the pain, from the joy?

We've all been there. We've all gone for weeks or months or years without paying attention to our emotional lives, at a great cost to our best selves. What would it look like if we gave ourselves permission to feel? What would it *feel* like?

The idea of the ~~I'm Fine~~ journal originated from the observation that the most common response to *"How are you?"* is very often *"I'm fine."*

"How are you?"
"Oh, I'm fine."
"How are your kids?"
"Oh, they're fine."
"How is your job?"
"Oh, it's fine."

We insist that everything's "fine," yet we are often hurting inside. Or maybe we want to share a celebratory moment but go with "fine" instead of sharing our true internal excitement to avoid appearing boastful. We cover and hide and put on the temporary mask of "fine." But as we've all experienced, there is something that doesn't seem authentic about "fine, fine, fine." It's when we begin to chisel away at the protective mechanisms and defensive layers we've put in place over the years that we can then discover the *real* feelings that are happening within our true selves. In the process, we will most certainly have an enriching, deepening experience of becoming more fully alive not only with ourselves, but also with those around us as we develop a deeper sensitivity to our own feelings.

Potentially, one of the most difficult pieces of using this journal will be just that—using it. If reflection and journaling are not currently part of your routine, acknowledge that and count yourself as a beginner. How refreshing to begin a new adventure! Know that in the beginning you may fail to write daily or forget about the journal completely. That is okay. You can begin again. The idea is to practice—in the way that works best for you, for your schedule and for your heart.

The other, maybe even more challenging task will be identifying your true, deep feelings. Actually *feeling* a particular feeling is hard work! It can be a long journey from our heads to our hearts. There have been many times when I've been unable to express clearly what I was feeling. Exploring our feelings is truly a sacred work, and an intimate work to be carried out with self-compassion and care. Sometimes the experience of fully expressing ourselves leads us to feel vulnerable and fully exposed. It can be difficult, even painful at times to explore our feelings, but my experience has been that it is truly worth it.

As we engage in this sacred work of identifying, feeling and expressing our feelings, it's helpful to remember that our feelings do not define us. Feelings come and feelings go. As much as possible, gaze upon your feelings without judgment. Bring to this experience an attitude of openness and adventure.

Journaling our feelings can resemble exploring a cave. As we journey farther into what's hidden, we might be surprised by unexpected discoveries, we might decide to push through and see what's next, or we might decide we've gone far enough for now and turn back. We might get a glimpse of something but decide not to touch it for the time being, or we might even decide to be still and sit with the experience for a moment. Exploration and discovery is an adventure. Consider yourself a pilgrim.

It is often said, "A sorrow shared is a sorrow cut in half, and a joy shared is a joy doubled." You may decide that the intensity level elicited by drawing and writing about your inner feelings is too high. Maybe it will be helpful to reach out and ask a friend or therapist to share the journey with you. My personal experience has proven that my load lightens and I experience a life-giving freedom when I have the courage to ask for help.

Your understanding of *you* is the journey you're about to take—may this journal be a light along your path. Let your words, your drawings, your expressions, your feelings, your tears, and your heart become fully alive as you *feel* your feelings here. May the experience be rich, deep and meaningful, and may you experience wholeness and healing on this journey of awakening.

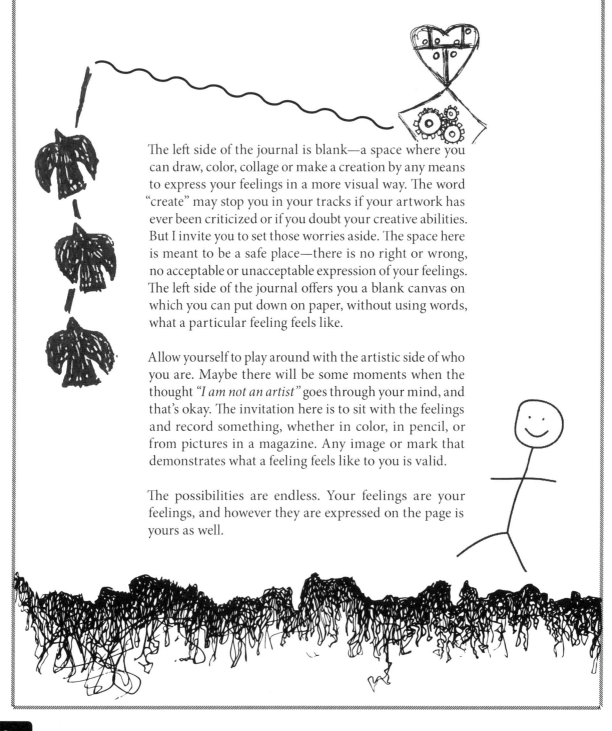

The left side of the journal is blank—a space where you can draw, color, collage or make a creation by any means to express your feelings in a more visual way. The word "create" may stop you in your tracks if your artwork has ever been criticized or if you doubt your creative abilities. But I invite you to set those worries aside. The space here is meant to be a safe place—there is no right or wrong, no acceptable or unacceptable expression of your feelings. The left side of the journal offers you a blank canvas on which you can put down on paper, without using words, what a particular feeling feels like.

Allow yourself to play around with the artistic side of who you are. Maybe there will be some moments when the thought *"I am not an artist"* goes through your mind, and that's okay. The invitation here is to sit with the feelings and record something, whether in color, in pencil, or from pictures in a magazine. Any image or mark that demonstrates what a feeling feels like to you is valid.

The possibilities are endless. Your feelings are your feelings, and however they are expressed on the page is yours as well.

For the RIGHT SIDE *of this journal...*

The right side of the journal is a space where you can begin to explore and express your feelings through writing. Here you can engage with your emotions and put words to what is waiting inside your heart for expression. Each page has a feeling word listed as a way to begin the process. You can go in alphabetical order and explore your feelings in that way or you can look at the table of feelings, pick the word that most describes how you are feeling at that moment, and begin to write. As much as you can, just let the feelings and the words flow. There is no need to worry about punctuation, grammar, or "proper" wording—just get those feelings on the page.

By using both the left and the right side of this journal you make use of your artistic and analytical abilities and open yourself to the possibility of a deeper integration of emotional health and all the parts of who you are. In Appendix A you'll find a list of additional feeling words followed by extra pages. You may choose to write in any feeling word on these pages—maybe even a feeling word that is not listed in the appendix. Appendix B offers a list of prompts and reflection questions that can be used to help you dig a little deeper, and in Appendix C you'll find various suggestions for ways to implement this journal. Appendix D contains some prompts using the poem, "The Guest House" by Jelaluddin Rumi, as a metaphorical way to observe your emotional inner world.

As you open the envelope of your heart, allow the space on the lines to be an invitation—a safe place for you to feel, to practice, to write, and to love yourself in a new way. The practice of awareness to our feelings is the goal, the journal is a tool.

TABLE OF FEELINGS

AFRAID

ALIVE

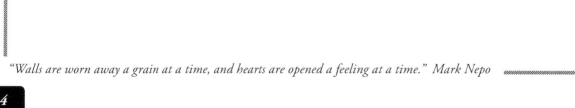

"Walls are worn away a grain at a time, and hearts are opened a feeling at a time." Mark Nepo

ANGRY

disastrous outcome
feelings of inadequacy/shame/guilt
feelings of loss/grief/awareness
    explicitly that relationship w/
    dad isn't what I hoped/expected
    - put me in bad position
    - no support
    - no accountability

So... it breed anxiety. about
    performance outcome, and
    wanting to do everything I could to
    succeed (over performing) so I
    wouldn't experience loss.
If can't rely on others, it's all
me. If it's all me, can't fail.
I'm in a Glue. So self worth a
extrinsicly driven.

Rather be in position of trusting others,
performing (not ours) and if not
successful - deal with feelings, boundaries,
accountability. Can be human, not
super human.
    To be human - doing the best I can
given the context - time/resources/relationships.

Self - compassion is critical
ok to fail/not do enough
do best I can w/out sacrificing
integrity, values.

APATHETIC

Piglet: *"How do you spell 'love'?"*
Pooh: *"You don't spell it—you feel it." A.A. Milne, Winne the Pooh*

APPRECIATED

"It is only by risking from one hour to another that we live at all." William James

BEAUTIFUL

"A world without color is like being human without feeling; both are distorted." Nawal Ghali

BEWILDERED

BITTER

BORED

BROKEN

"We all have the extraordinary coded inside us, waiting to be released." Jean Houston

CALM

CHEERFUL

"Wisdom begins in wonder." Socrates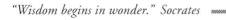

CONFIDENT

CONFUSED

"Beauty is the illumination of your soul." John O'Donohue

CONTENT

"I am still learning." Michelangelo

"We do not grow absolutely, chronologically.
We grow sometimes in one dimension, and not in another; unevenly.
We grow partially. We are relative. We are mature in one realm, childish in another.
The past, present, and future mingle and pull us backward, forward, or fix us in the present.
We are made up of layers, cells, constellations." Anaïs Nin

DEPRESSED

DEVASTATED

DISAPPOINTED

"There is a great deal of pain in life and perhaps the only pain that can be avoided is the pain that comes from trying to avoid pain." R.D. Laing

DISCERNING

DISCOURAGED

"The beginnings of all things are weak and tender." Michel de Montaigne

DISTANT

"I hope you will go out and let stories happen to you, and that you will work them, water them with your blood and tears and your laughter till they bloom, till you yourself burst into bloom." Clarissa Pinkola Estés

ENERGETIC

EXCITED

"What lies behind us and what lies before us are tiny matters, compared to what lies within us." Ralph Waldo Emerson

FAITHFUL

FRUSTRATED

"A broken heart is much like a broken rib—from the outside everything looks fine, but on the inside every breath hurts." *Anonymous*

GRATEFUL

"Out of your vulnerabilities will come your strength." Sigmund Freud

82

GUILTY

HAPPY

"I've learned that people will forget what you said, people will forget what you did, but people will never forget how you made them feel." Maya Angelou

HATEFUL

HELPLESS

"Be patient towards all that is unsolved in your heart,
and learn to love the questions themselves." Rainer Maria Rilke

HOPEFUL

HOSTILE

"The journey between what you once were and who you are now
becoming is where the dance of life really takes place." Barbara De Angelis

resting 23 !!

never really seen
never only an expression of
seen their desires - approval
their desires - approval performance

never seen for
who I really was
or how I felt

felt small to be
like a bug to be
squished
felt not important, seen,
felt not important, seen,
valued

Not doing
feelings is an
insult. That
lack was an even tho not my fault -
injury. Affected felt responsible
me for 5   felt anger f hurt f shame?
decider.   embarrassment at
                         situation but

Just like
avoidance or   an also felt hurt @ my father - how could
distancing St - anger, but   you, why were
aggressive act -   you, where were you - why were
has deep impact   you not taking care of me, where
                    was your awareness of me?
                   Not important, not valued -
                   scaffolded onto other past
                   things - death threats, arson
                   attempt, cannery -

these were deep wounds - never acknowledged,
never addressed, never resolved, no reckoning -

HURT

"People have said, 'Don't cry' to other people…
I'd rather hear them say, 'Go ahead and cry. I'm here to be with you'." Mr. Rogers

IMPORTANT

INADEQUATE

INSECURE

"May we all grow in grace and peace, and not neglect the silence
that is printed in the center of our being. It will not fail us." Thomas Merton

INTIMATE

"The voyage of discovery is not in seeking new landscapes, but in having new eyes." Marcel Proust

LONELY

"Owning our own story can be hard but not nearly as difficult as spending our lives running from it." Brené Brown

LOVING

NERVOUS

"There came a time when the risk to remain tight in a bud was more painful than the risk it took to bloom." Anaïs Nin

NURTURING

OPTIMISTIC

"Emotions are the language of the soul.
They are the cry that gives the heart a voice.
To understand our deepest passions and convictions,
we must learn to listen to the cry of the soul." Dr. Dan Allender

POWERFUL

PROUD

"*The best and most beautiful things in the world cannot be seen or even touched—they must be felt with the heart.*" Anne Sullivan as remembered by Helen Keller

RELAXED

RESPECTED

SAD

"There is a time for everything and a season for every activity under heaven:…
a time to weep and a time to laugh, a time to mourn and a time to dance." Ecclesiastes 3:1,4

SATISFIED

SCARED

"Vulnerability is a skill that opens up the heart for love to take root." Dr. Henry Cloud

SELFISH

"I would love to live like a river flows, carried by the surprise of its own unfolding." John O'Donohue

SENSUOUS

SHAME

"Thousands of emotions well up inside me throughout the day. They are released when I dance." Abraham Lincoln

SUBMISSIVE

TENDER

"It is with the heart that one sees rightly; what is essential is invisible to the eye." Antoine de Saint-Exupéry, *The Little Prince*

THOUGHTFUL

TIRED

TRUSTED

"Anybody can become angry—that is easy, but to be angry with the right person and to the right degree and at the right time and for the right purpose, and in the right way—that is not within everybody's power and is not easy." *Aristotle*

UPTIGHT

VALUABLE

"But feelings can't be ignored, no matter how unjust or ungrateful they seem." Anne Frank

VULNERABLE

WEARY

"The best way out is always through." Robert Frost

WELL

WORRIED

"Even the darkest night will end and the sun will rise." Victor Hugo, Les Misérables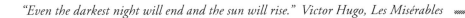

A

able
abnormal
accepted
accomplished
affectionate
aggressive
alone
ambivalent
annoyed
apologetic
apprehensive
arrogant
awe
awesome
awful
awkward

B

bad
behind
best
betrayed
better
blah
bleak
blessed
blissful
blue
brave

C

capable
cared for
caring
cautious
certain
cherished

close
clueless
cold
comfortable
compelled
competent
complete
concerned
contemptuous
cool
crabby
crappy
crazy
crushed
curious

D

dangerous
dead
defeated
dejected
delighted
dependent
desirable
despairing
desperate
determined
different
dirty
disgusted
disheartened
distrustful
doubtful
down
dumb

E

eager

ecstatic
empty
enraged
enthusiastic
envious
exasperated
exhausted

F

fascinated
fat
fearful
festive
fine
foolish
forgiving
fragile
frantic
frazzled
friendly
fulfilled
full

G

generous
glad
good
great
grief
grounded
grumpy

H

harassed
heartbroken
heartless
high
hopeless

horrible
horrified
hot
humorous
hungry
hysterical

I

ignored
ill
impatient
impotent
incompetent
indecisive
indifferent
inhibited
innocent
insignificant
interested
intuitive
irate
irritated
isolated

J

jealous
joyous
jubilant
jumpy

L

lazy
light
lost
lovable
loved
lovestruck

loyal
lucky

M

mad
mean
melancholy
miserable
misunderstood
moody
muddled

N

naked
needed
needy
nice
normal
numb

O

obligated
obstinate
okay
old
on edge
outraged
overwhelmed

P

pained
panic
panicky
paranoid
passionate
pathetic
peaceful
pensive

pessimistic
phony
pissed
playful
pleased
poisonous
prejudiced
preoccupied
pressured
pretty
protective
provoked
prudish
puzzled

R

ready
regretful
relieved
remorseful
resentful
reserved
responsive

S

safe
sarcastic
secure
self-concious
self-reliant
separated
serene
sexy
sheepish
shitty
shocked
shy
sick

sick and tired
silly
skeptical
small
smug
sorry
special
stimulated
strange
stressed
strong
stubborn
stuck
stupid
successful
supportive
sure
surprised
suspicious
sympathetic

T

taxing
tense
terrible
terrified
thankful
threatened
thrilled
tired
touchy
troubled

U

ugly
unappreciated
unattractive
uncertain

uncomfortable
undecided
understanding
understood
uneasy
unfulfilled
unhappy
unique
unloved
upset
used
useless

V

victimized
violated

W

wanted
warm
weak
weird
wishy-washy
withdrawn
witty
wonderful
worn out
worse
worthwhile
wrong

Y

young
youthful

Z

zealous
zen

Prompts

1. If I could allow myself to feel _____, I would...

2. When I am with _____ (name), I often feel _____.

3. If I weren't feeling so _____, what else would I be feeling?

4. If I were free of my _____, I would be feeling _____.

5. When I was in the situation of feeling _____, I also felt _____.

6. I realize my feeling of _____ is not to hurt me, but to let me know myself more.

7. In the past, I have felt _____ when...

8. A time in my childhood when I felt _____ was...

9. When I felt _____ as a child, I often _____ (name of behavior or action).

10. When I feel _____ I often...

11. When I feel _____ I never...

12. If people knew I was feeling _____ they would be surprised.

13. When I was a teenager, I remember feeling _____ about...

14. I never feel _____ because...

15. When I cry, I feel _____ because...

16. If people saw me cry, I would...

17. I never cry because I feel...

18. If I ever did cry, I would feel...

19. What are the tears about?

20. I might have felt better if I cried when I was feeling _____ because...

21. When I laugh, I feel _____ because...

22. I never laugh because I feel...

23. I have a difficult time feeling _____ because...

24. When I feel _____ I think about...

25. It takes courage to feel _____.

26. I feel vulnerable when I feel _____.

27. I desire to give myself permission to feel _____.

28. I feel _____ when...

29. I try to hide my feeling of _____ because...

30. I don't mind sharing my feeling of _____ because...

31. I wish I could feel more _____ about...

32. When I want to honor my feeling of _____, I...

33. It feels _____ to open up the box of memories about...

34. Sometimes I stay busy to keep from feeling _____ because...

35. I sometimes don't take time to feel _____ because...

36. An unpleasant feeling for me is _____ because...

37. When I try to recall memories about feeling _____, I remember...

38. It really surprised me when I felt _____ at _____ (name of event).

39. Sometimes I try to avoid feeling _____ like when...

40. I feel _____ when _____.
    Repeat sentence multiple times with same feeling word. (*For example: I feel overwhelmed when I think about cleaning out the garage. I feel overwhelmed when I get up in the mornings. I feel overwhelmed when I see ads about retirement. I feel overwhelmed when I think of my mother's death.*)

Reflection Questions

1. What is happening in me right now? Can I write more about that feeling?

2. What is stirring in my heart right now?

3. How do I respond to feeling _____?

4. What is the next question that wants to be asked?

5. What would happen if I sat with the feeling of _____?

6. Am I feeling fully expressed or fully exposed and why?

7. What important message is my feeling of _____ telling me?

8. Where do I find great _____ in my life?

9. What causes _____ in my life?

10. How do I experience my feelings through the senses of touch, taste, sound, smell & sight?

11. What first happened that made me feel this way?

12. What am I feeling right now? How strong is that feeling?

13. Where do I feel _____ in my body?

14. What do I understand or know about the feeling I am experiencing?

15. What feelings paralyze me and why?

On Your Own

1. Proceed in the alphabetical order of the journal and write/draw about an experience you've had with the particular feeling either now or in the past.

2. Look at the Table of Feelings list and choose the feeling that is applicable at this very moment for you. Turn to that page in the journal and write.

3. Consider memories. Ask yourself when you experienced a feeling in the past. Recognize the feeling in the past and let that help you get a handle on how you feel in the present.

4. Explore your emotions by writing for 10 minutes each day for a period of time. Remember, beginning something new is challenging.

5. Look through photos to recognize a moment of feeling. Let that picture be a prompt for you of a "feeling moment" that you would like to draw or write about.

6. As you become more in tune with your emotional self, you may find yourself reflecting on your feelings when you do not have your journal with you. No worries! Just write or draw your feelings on whatever is at hand—a scrap of paper, a napkin at the restaurant, the barf bag on the plane—and tape the writing into your journal at a later time.

7. Experiment with coloring or drawing for 10 minutes each day for a set period.

8. Come to the journal once a week and discover the depths of your feelings by intentionally focusing some time each week to discover new pieces of your heart.

9. Explore your own creative way to write/draw/experience the journal.

10. Think of a significant event—moving to a new home/city/state, retirement, transitioning from high school to college, wedding, death, promotion, divorce, diagnosis, adopting, birth of a child, etc.—any event can have a range of emotions attached to it. Write/draw how you feel about this particular event and the change that is occurring within you because of the event.

11. Choose an area that you seem to be struggling with and devote the journal to that. For example, if you are struggling with your career or your career choice or the office politics, use the journal to delve deeper into the struggle.

12. Ponder and write a page or a paragraph: What is the life map of your feelings story? What did you feel at age 5, 10, 15, 20, 25, etc.?

13. Make collages instead of drawing and tape or glue them into the journal.

14. Think about what color you might attach to a specific feeling.

15. Collect quotes that you like regarding various feelings and add them to your journal as you discover the quote.

16. What music stirs you to feel? Journal about your feelings under the appropriate feeling page as you become aware of the emotion the music pulls out of you. Perhaps write down meaningful song lyrics or make yourself a playlist.

17. Pair the journal writing with a breathing exercise. What feeling do you want to breathe in? What feeling do you want to breathe out?

18. If you become aware of a feeling while out on a walk, pick up a flower or leaf or another object that catches your eye and place it on the left side of the journal as a reminder of the feeling you felt as you walked.

19. Experiment. Have fun. Mess up. Cry. Laugh. Try something new. Go back. Feel now. Look forward. Mess up again. Listen to yourself. Go deep. Come back to the surface. Go deep again. Be a beginner. Discover. Cry. Laugh. Sigh. Breathe. Try. Try again. Enjoy. Grow. Love deeper. Listen more. Journal the journey.

With Others

*Practice empathy here—true sharing of feelings is only safe in a safe environment. Try not to use the feelings journal as a manipulative weapon to prove a point, feel superior to another, etc. Just like a hammer, the journal can be a tool or a weapon—it can be used to build up or tear down. Be aware of offering love to your fellow pilgrims. One of my favorite anonymous quotes to keep in mind in group settings is, "**Feelings are everywhere—be gentle.**"*

1. Gather with a small community of friends or with a partner once a week or every other week and together explore the feelings you feel safe to share about. This is a great way to incorporate accountability into the process of discovery.

2. As a family—even if the children are little—begin teaching and exploring the value of feelings by writing, drawing and sharing together as a family.

3. Get a journal for each member of the family and once a week have a "Feelings Feast" where each person shares something out of their journal for the week.

4. With your partner or close friend, deepen the conversations by first writing/drawing in the journal and then listening to one another's sharing about what each has written/drawn.

The poem "The Guest House" by Jelaluddin Rumi, found at the beginning of this book, can be used as a tool to help us recognize, understand and feel our feelings. As we ponder our own interiority, we may discover that although temporary, our feelings are truly important guests, worthy of honor. After reading "The Guest House," try an act of inner hospitality by opening your mind and heart to all the guests (feelings) knocking at the door of your guest house. Then consider these questions and see where they lead you. I invite you to journal your response to the questions with the hope that they help you welcome all the guests waiting on the doorstep.

1. What feeling guest automatically gets the welcome mat in my life?

2. Which feeling is a regular "drop-in" guest for me?

3. What would it look like if I treated my feeling of _____ with honor as I would a beloved guest?

4. How can I welcome a range of guests without being swept away by them?

5. What happens when an awkward feeling comes knocking at the door? How can I welcome this guest into my life?

6. What does clutter in my guest house look like?

7. Have I ignored a knock at the door and pretended not to be home? If so, why? Who was I expecting? Why were they not welcome?

8. How can opening the guest house be a virtuous struggle?

9. What feeling guest do I feel uncomfortable with?

10. Is my guest house so well organized that no messy feelings are allowed? How can I make space for them?

11. What unexpected feeling guest showed up today for me?

12. Where is the key to open/close the door to my feelings?

13. What changes would need to occur if I allowed the feeling of _____ into the house?

14. What feeling guest am I hiding from?

15. How does my perfectionism keep me from opening the door to a feeling guest?

16. Is the guest house too noisy to recognize new guests that may be arriving? How can I still be attentive to that new guest?

17. What is in the cellar of the guest house?

18. What's the last feeling guest I'd like to see on my doorstep?

19. How can I be vulnerable and have courage to ask the feeling of _____ to leave?

20. Which feeling guest do I wish would leave so that I could put everything back as it was before that guest arrived?

21. How can I be open to the feeling of _____ that is knocking at the door?

22. Are there any disjointed or displaced parts of the guest house?

23. How do we welcome the feelings that are strangers to us?

24. What makes me want to escape out the backdoor?

25. What windows need to be unlocked or opened to let in some light?

26. Do I wish the feeling guest of _____ would leave now? What if they can't?

27. What guests require me to tiptoe around the house?

28. What feeling has been boarded up? What needs to happen for it to be released?

THANK YOU

A heart full of gratitude to those who have helped this journal come to be...

A NOTE OF THANKS FROM DIANNE

Thanks to my precious family Roger, Justin, Jill and Brent—you all are such an amazing encouragement! You listening to my crazy ideas and then supporting them with gusto are part of what makes my life beautiful. Thanks to Monica—what an incredible journey this has been. You are a talented woman who has a heart for excellence. Thanks to Catherine for editing the journal—you are brilliant! What a gift to know you. Thanks to Nawal and Kathy for teaching me how to understand my feelings more—this journal could be dedicated to you. Thank you to all of my family, friends and clients; many of you have helped in your own special way. Thank you God, for waking me up in the middle of the night with ideas like the I'm Fine journal; may we each dig deep to discover the beauty and depth of the feelings You have created within us. ❀

A NOTE OF THANKS FROM MONICA

If you would have told me a year ago that I would be designing and laying out books I would have probably laughed. I think I did laugh a little in that first meeting with you, Dianne. Thank you for taking me on anyway and believing that I could be a part of this team. I have already learned so much from and with you. To my eagle-eyed, design-loving, grammar savvy friends who took time to examine and encourage—Brian, Billy & Emily—thank you, you're amazing. To my incredibly wise and knowledgeable teachers—Luann & Joe—thank you for teaching me everything I know about typography just in the nick of time! And of course to my family and friends, you know who you are, you have supported me so unequivocally in this new endeavor and I know you're the reason I've been able to keep growing. Thank you, from the bottom of my heart. ❀

ABOUT US

DIANNE MORRIS JONES is a Licensed Mental Health Counselor (LMHC) and a Certified Daring Way™ Facilitator (CDWF-C) practicing at Family Legacy Counseling in Des Moines, Iowa. She has a degree in Family Finance from Texas Tech University and a master's degree in Counseling from West Texas A&M University. Dianne is an energetic and creative person who approaches life and her professional counseling with an enthusiasm for growth in wholehearted living. She practices individual and couples therapy from a mindful, cognitive behavioral approach. Dianne is multi-faceted in her practice, incorporating various learning environments in addition to one-on-one counseling. Her clinical focus includes working with depression, anxiety, relationship issues, trauma, and life transitions.

Dianne specializes in helping clients embrace their authenticity and encourages clients to create lives that reflect their values and passions. She supports holistic living in her approach by being intentional to view life through emotional, physical, spiritual, financial, intellectual and relational perspectives. In addition to being a Certified Laughter Yoga Instructor, Dianne has extensive training in Spiritual Direction and the Enneagram. The Daring Way™ is a highly experiential methodology based on the research of Dr. Brené Brown that focuses on developing shame resilience skills and developing a courage practice that transforms the way we live, love, parent and lead.

Dianne enjoys friends, outdoor adventures, photography and spending time with their adult children, Justin and Jill. Dianne and her husband, Roger, live in West Des Moines, Iowa. **«**

www.diannemorrisjones.com **« ❀ »** www.daringindesmoines.com

MONICA GHALI is an aspiring recognizer and creator of beautiful things and a lover of story. After receiving her Bachelor of Arts from Taylor University Monica moved to Lima, Peru where her work in non-profit pushed her to meet incredible people, face into many interesting challenges, and experience the world in a new way. Her work there eventually led to a discovery of her desire to explore creative fields and their connection to advocacy. She is now living in Omaha, Nebraska where she just finished a fellowship at the Union for Contemporary Art, is soaking in the wisdom of the creative community, and working as a freelance designer. You can find her at monicaghali.com. **«**

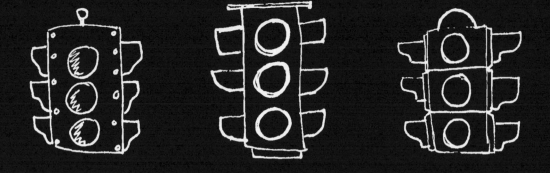

Made in the USA
Middletown, DE
11 January 2020